SAFARI ADVENTURE

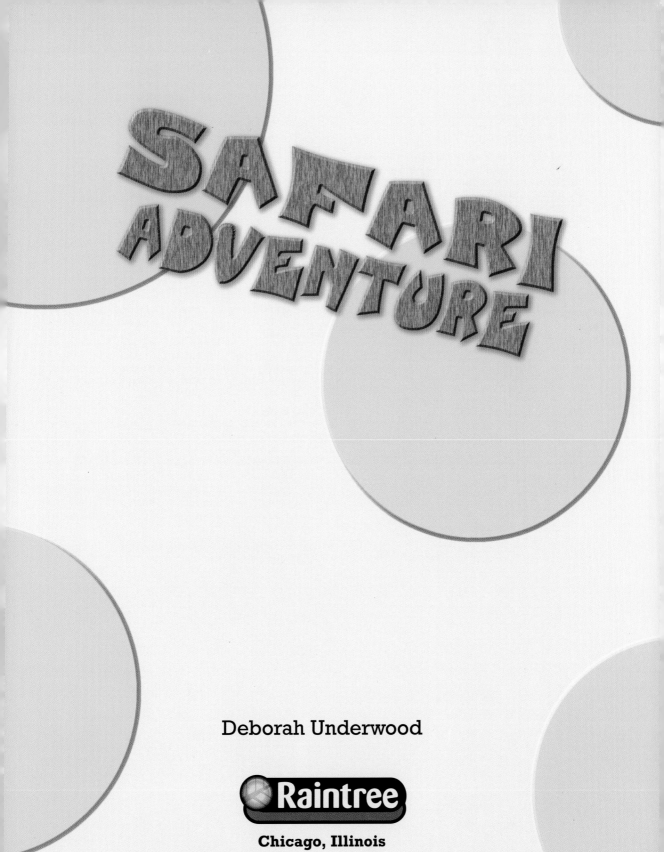

Deborah Underwood

Raintree

Chicago, Illinois

Designed by Philippa Jenkins and Q2A Creative

Printed by Leo Paper Group

12 11 10 09 08
10 9 8 7 6 5 4 3 2 1

**Library of Congress Cataloging-in-Publication
Data**
Underwood, Deborah.
    Safari adventure / Deborah Underwood.
      p. cm.
    Includes bibliographical references and index.
    ISBN-13: 978-1-4109-2843-6 (library binding)
    ISBN-10: 1-4109-2843-8 (library binding)
    ISBN-13: 978-1-4109-2860-3 (pbk.)
    ISBN-10: 1-4109-2860-8 (pbk.)
1. Mathematics--Juvenile literature. 2. Mathematics-
-Graphic methods--Juvenile literature. 3. Charts,
diagrams, etc--Juvenile literature. I. Title.
    QA40.5.U53 2007
    510--dc22
                                          2006102805

Acknowledgments
The author and publisher are grateful to the
following for permission to reproduce copyright
material: Alamy/Stock Connection/Galen Rowell/
Mountain Light p. **5**; Alamy pp. **16–17** (Bob
Handelman), **18–19** (Tim Graham); Corbis/DLILLC
p. **6–7**; Corbis p. **8** (Brian A. Vikander); Duncan
Gilbert p. **12–13**; FLPA/Minden Pictures/JH
Editorial p. **24–25** (Cyril Ruoso); Getty Images/
Gallo Images p. **15** (Dave Hamman); Getty Images/
National Geographic p. **26** (Medford Taylor); Getty
Images/Photographer's Choice p.**10–11** (Laurence
Monneret); Getty Images/Stone p. **20–21** (Michael
Busselle), **22–23** (J Sneesby/B Wilkins).

Cover photograph of an African elephant (*Loxodonta
africana*), with calf reproduced with permission of
Photolibrary.com/Martyn Colbeck.

Illustrations by Jeff Edwards.

The publishers would like to thank Nancy Harris and
Harold Pratt for their assistance in the preparation of
this book.

Every effort has been made to contact copyright
holders of any material reproduced in this book. Any
omissions will be rectified in subsequent printings if
notice is given to the publishers.

Disclaimer
All the Internet addresses (URLs) given in this book
were valid at the time of going to press. However,
due to the dynamic nature of the Internet, some
addresses may have changed, or sites may have
changed or ceased to exist since publication. While
the author and publishers regret any inconvenience
this may cause readers, no responsibility for any such
changes can be accepted by either the author or the
publishers.

It is recommended that adults supervise children on
the Internet.

Contents

Some words are printed in bold, **like this**. You can find out what they mean on page 30. You can also look in the box at the bottom of the page where they first appear.

Africa at Last!

The Sun rises over the grassy plains. The sky is bright orange. A lion roars in the distance. You are in Africa!

Giraffes. Zebras. Crocodiles. You hope to see them all in this game park. But this is not a vacation. You are here to collect **data**. Data means pieces of information.

You will watch animals and write down what you see. You will put your data into **tables**. Tables help you arrange data in a clear way.

Then, you will find the best way to show your data to others. You will use the data to make **graphs**. The graphs will help you see patterns in your data. The things you learn may help the animals here.

Your guide pulls up in a jeep. You hop in. Your safari adventure is beginning!

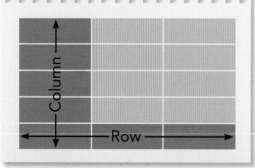

Tables have rows and columns. The rows go across. The columns go up and down.

data pieces of information
graph picture that shows data
table chart that organizes data

On safari

The word *safari* means "journey" in the African language Swahili.

↑ *Sunrise is peaceful in the Serengeti National Park.*

Water Puzzle

Your jeep bounces up and down on the rough roads. Dust flies into the air. It is the dry season here. Animals gather where there is water.

You park by a water hole. The water looks dirty. It smells terrible. Insects buzz above it.

A clear spring bubbles from the ground nearby. Tall grass grows on one side. This water looks much cleaner.

These gazelles gather near water in the dry season.

horizontal flat
tally mark line that stands for something you are counting
vertical upright

Are animals drinking the dirty water? You will watch and find out. You need a place to write down what you see. You draw a **table** on your notepad.

A zebra drinks from the water hole. You make a mark in the water-hole row. A buffalo drinks from the spring. You make a mark in the spring row. Each mark is called a **tally mark**.

After an hour your table looks like this:

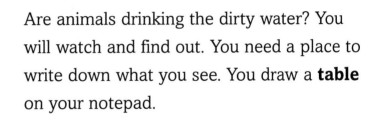

| Animals Drinking from Water Hole | ⵏⵏⵏ ⵏⵏⵏ ⵏⵏⵏ ⵏⵏⵏ ⵏⵏⵏ ⵏⵏⵏ ⵏⵏⵏ |
| Animals Drinking from Spring | ‖‖‖ |

Tally marks

Tally marks are often made in groups of five. This makes them easier to count. The first four marks are **vertical** (upright) and the fifth is **horizontal** (flat).

Water danger

You draw a **pie chart**. Pie charts are circles divided into pieces. This pie chart shows all the animals you saw drinking. The large piece (blue) shows animals that drank from the water hole. The small piece (red) shows animals that drank from the spring.

Your guide does not understand the chart. Aha! You know why. Your chart needs a title and **labels**. Labels tell what each part of the chart means. Without labels, a chart does not make sense.

Most animals are drinking from the dirty water hole. But why?

A gazelle walks to the spring. A lion pounces! The lion was hiding in the grass by the spring. The gazelle dashes off. No wonder most animals do not drink there.

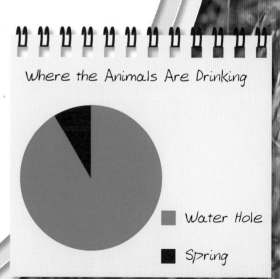

Where the Animals Are Drinking

Water Hole

Spring

8

label words that tell what part of a graph means
pie chart graph showing what parts make up a whole

This lion hopes he has found a meal.

Circle or pie?

Pie charts can be called circle **graphs**. But most people call them pie charts because they look like pies.

Giraffes and Jeeps

The next day you drive to a group of trees. Giraffes often come here to eat. Park visitors come to watch them.

Each jeep parks here for half an hour. Some park very close to the trees. Are the jeeps scaring the giraffes away from their food?

You will collect two types of **data**:
- You will see how far away each jeep parks.
- You will count the giraffes that eat while each jeep is there.

The first jeep arrives. It parks 10 feet (3 meters) away from the trees. Two giraffes come to nibble leaves while the jeep is there. You write this down.

In an hour the next jeep arrives. It parks 20 feet (6 meters) away. This time you count three giraffes.

Giraffes like to eat the leaves of acacia trees.

After several hours, your **table** looks like this:

Distance of Jeep from Trees	Number of Giraffes that Come to Eat
10 feet (3 meters)	2
20 feet (6 meters)	3
30 feet (9 meters)	16
40 feet (12 meters)	18
50 feet (15 meters)	19

Now, you have your data. But a **graph** will help you see patterns more easily.

Graphing giraffes

You make a **bar graph**. Bar graphs compare information. The numbers at the bottom show how far away the jeeps were parked. The numbers on the left show how many animals came to eat.

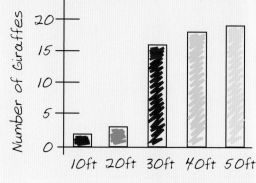

How Jeep Distance Affects Giraffe Eating

The first jeep parked 10 feet (3 meters) away. Two giraffes ate while it was there. The first mark on the left side of your **graph** means five animals. You draw the bar a little less than halfway to the mark.

The bar graph contains the same **data** as your **table**. But the graph is a picture. It helps you see patterns.

If jeeps are 20 feet (6 meters) or closer, few giraffes come. Lots of giraffes come when the jeeps stay at least 30 feet (9 meters) away. It will be better for the giraffes if the jeeps stay at least 30 feet (9 meters) away.

Big bones

Giraffes have seven neck bones. So do humans!

bar graph   graph that uses rectangle-shaped bars to compare data

Giraffes use their 18-inch (46-centimeter) tongues to strip leaves from branches.

Cat Count

A lot of big cats live in the park. Today, you will count the cats in one area. You want to see how the lions are doing. Last year many lions died. You hope the number of lions is growing.

You make a **table** to help keep count. You could put the animal names in the first column. But this time you put the animal names in the first row. Either way will work fine.

Your jeep travels slowly. You look carefully. Bingo! You see a group of lions. There are two females and five cubs. You **record** (write down) that you saw seven lions.

Lions	Cheetahs	Leopards
2 + 5		

The day is over. You add up your numbers. Your table looks like this:

Lions	Cheetahs	Leopards
2 + 5 + 3 = 10	2 + 3 + 2 = 7	1 + 1 + 1 = 3

At camp, you make a **bar graph**. This time the bars will go across, not up and down. Either way shows the same **data**.

Lions live in groups called prides.

record write down

Number of Cats This Year

Leopards

Cheetahs

Lions

0   10   20

Number of Cats

Lion lunches

Female lions do most of the hunting. But males get to share the food they catch!

Good news for lions

Your guide hands you a **table**. It is from last year's cat count in the same area.

Last Year's Cat Count		
Lions	Cheetahs	Leopards
2	8	3

→ Cheetahs have spotted coats that help them hide in the grass.

double bar graph   graph that uses two bars to compare two kinds of data

You use this **data** to make a **double bar graph**. A double bar graph shows two different types of data. You can use it to compare this year's count with last year's count. You use a different color for each year. This makes the **graph** easy to understand.

Number of Cats This Year and Last Year

Leopards

Cheetahs

Lions

■ Last Year

■ This Year

0   10   20

Number of Cats

The number of leopards and cheetahs has stayed about the same. But there are many more lions.

You collected data for only one day. You looked in only one part of the park. People will do more cat counts later. But so far it looks like good news for the lions.

Crocs on Rocks

Today, you will travel to a river. At least it used to be a river. This is the end of the dry season. The river has become a string of water holes. But Nile crocodiles still live there!

Crocs use sunlight to keep warm. They use water and mud to keep cool. You will keep track of how many crocs sun themselves. You will count the crocs each hour.

Watching crocs is fun, but do not get too close!

King-sized crocs

Many Nile crocodiles grow to be 16 feet (5 meters) long.

Your guide parks the jeep at the edge of the water hole. It is 8 a.m. Eight crocs lie in the sun. You write that in your **table**. At 9 a.m., you hear a plop! A croc slips into the muddy water. There are seven left. You write that in your table.

At the end of the day, your table looks like this:

Time	Crocs on Shore
8 a.m.	8
9 a.m.	7
10 a.m.	5
11 a.m.	2
noon	1
1 p.m.	0
2 p.m.	0
3 p.m.	2
4 p.m.	3
5 p.m.	5
6 p.m.	7

Getting in line

Back at camp, you make a **line graph**. Line graphs show how one thing affects another. They are often used to show how things change over time. This graph shows how the number of crocs on shore changes with the time of day.

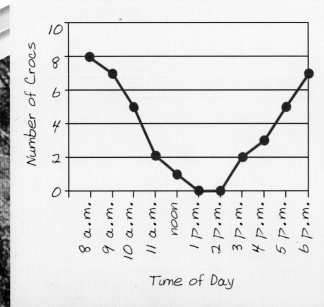

Number of Crocs on the Shore

line graph   graph that uses a line to show how one thing affects another

It is cool in the morning. The crocs come out to bask in the Sun. Then, the air heats up. The crocs cool off in the water. They come to shore again as the air cools.

Many visitors want to see the crocs. When would it be best for them to come?

In the middle of the day, it is hot. Your graph shows the crocs are in the water then. They are hard to see. So, visitors should come early or late in the day. It is cooler then. That is when the crocs come out to sun themselves.

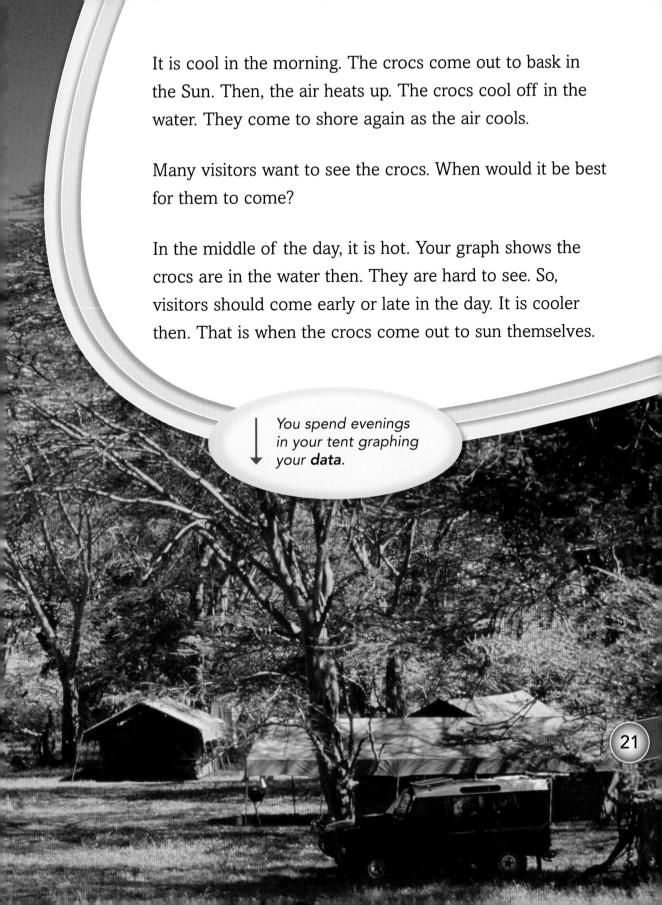

*You spend evenings in your tent graphing your **data**.*

Bug Bites

While you watch giraffes and crocs eat, you get eaten up—by bugs! Elephants roll in mud to keep bugs away. You would rather use bug spray.

You wonder when the bugs are the most active. You also wonder which bug spray is best. Your guide uses one kind. You use a different kind.

You and your guide each **record** (write down) when you get bites.

Time	Guide's Bug Bites	My Bug Bites
3–4 p.m.	0	1
4–5 p.m.	1	3
5–6 p.m.	2	4
6–7 p.m.	4	8
7–8 p.m.	4	7
8–9 p.m.	2	3
9–10 p.m.	0	1

Elephants roll in mud to avoid bugs.

double line graph line graph that compares two sets of data

You use a **double line graph** to show your **data**. A double line graph has two lines. Double line graphs can show how two things change over time.

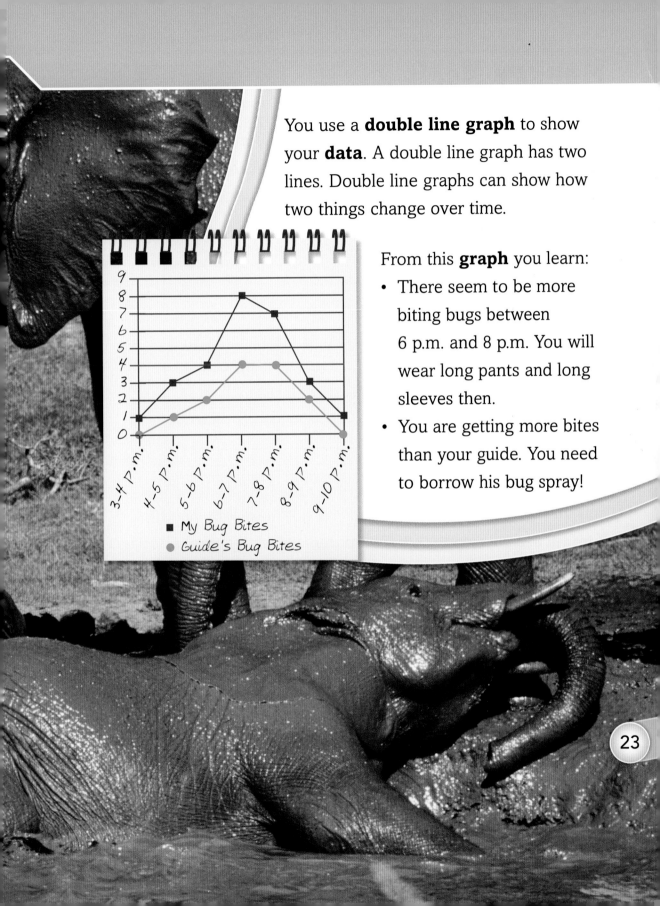

9
8
7
6
5
4
3
2
1
0

3-4 p.m.
4-5 p.m.
5-6 p.m.
6-7 p.m.
7-8 p.m.
8-9 p.m.
9-10 p.m.

■ My Bug Bites
● Guide's Bug Bites

From this **graph** you learn:
• There seem to be more biting bugs between 6 p.m. and 8 p.m. You will wear long pants and long sleeves then.
• You are getting more bites than your guide. You need to borrow his bug spray!

Monkey Meals

A group of trees grows near your camp. Baboons and monkeys eat the leaves. Which kind of animal eats there the most? You watch and write down your **data** in a **table**.

Time	Baboons Eating from Trees	Monkeys Eating from Trees	Total Animals Eating from Trees
8–10 a.m.	2	8	10
10 a.m.–noon	6	13	19
noon–2 p.m.	0	0	0
2–4 p.m.	5	0	5
4–6 p.m.	7	20	27
6–8 p.m.	0	21	21
Total	20	62	82

You make a **graph**. This time you will not draw it by hand. You will use your computer. Computers can draw graphs quickly. All you need to do is put in the data.

First, the computer draws a **pie chart**.

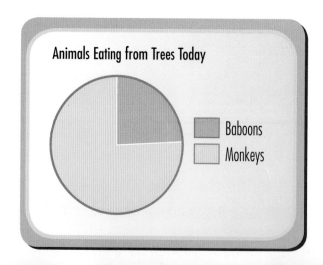

Leaves are a big part of the colobus monkey's diet.

More monkeys than baboons came to the tree today. The pie chart makes this easy to see.

But you decide you want to show something else. You want to show exactly how many animals came. You tell the computer to draw a **bar graph**.

Animals Eating from Trees Today

Baboons eat a lot of things. But these monkeys eat mostly leaves. A lot of monkeys spent time in the trees today. It looks like these trees are an important food source for them.

Lightning Strike!

Rain pounds on your tent in the night. The dry season is over. You see a flash of light. You hear an ear-splitting boom and a crack! Lightning has struck a tree nearby.

In the morning you go outside. An enormous branch has dropped to the ground. It blocks a park road.

When should park staff remove the broken branch? You get yesterday's **data**. Your computer makes a **line graph**.

↓ The Sun sets on the Serengeti.

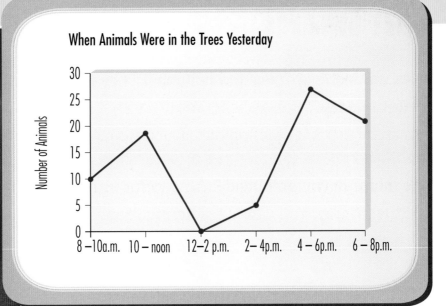

When Animals Were in the Trees Yesterday

Number of Animals

30
25
20
15
10
5
0

8 – 10a.m.   10 – noon   12 – 2 p.m.   2 – 4p.m.   4 – 6p.m.   6 – 8p.m.

You think they should remove the branch between noon and 2 p.m. Then they will not disturb many animals.

It is time to go home. You will miss Africa. You will miss the animals. But you have graphed a lot of data. Park staff will use your **graphs**. The graphs will help them make choices. The choices will help keep the animals safe and healthy.

You settle into your sleeping bag. Monkeys chatter and insects chirp. You drift off to sleep. You dream of the blueberry pie you will eat at home. All those **pie charts** made you hungry!

Chart Smarts

Tables are made of rows and columns. They help you arrange your **data** neatly.

Graphs and charts are pictures of data. They help you see relationships between things. Each type of graph shows data in a different way. You can use different graphs to show the same data.

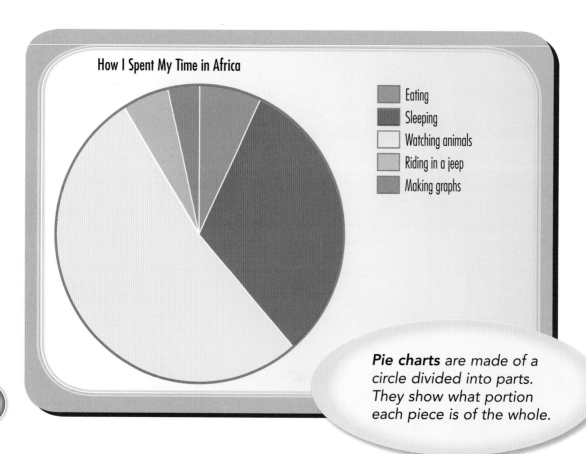

How I Spent My Time in Africa

- Eating
- Sleeping
- Watching animals
- Riding in a jeep
- Making graphs

Pie charts are made of a circle divided into parts. They show what portion each piece is of the whole.

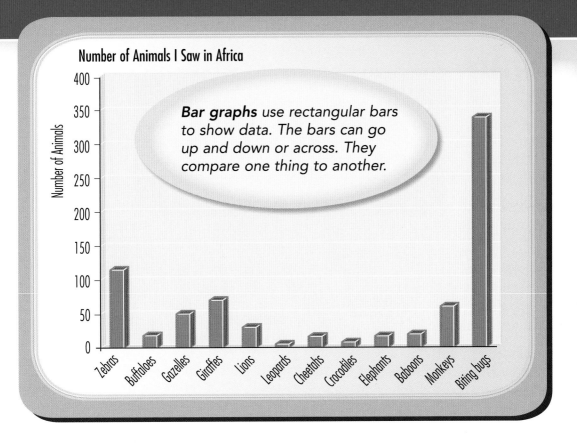

Number of Animals I Saw in Africa

Bar graphs use rectangular bars to show data. The bars can go up and down or across. They compare one thing to another.

Number of Animals

Zebras, Buffaloes, Gazelles, Giraffes, Lions, Leopards, Cheetahs, Crocodiles, Elephants, Baboons, Monkeys, Biting bugs

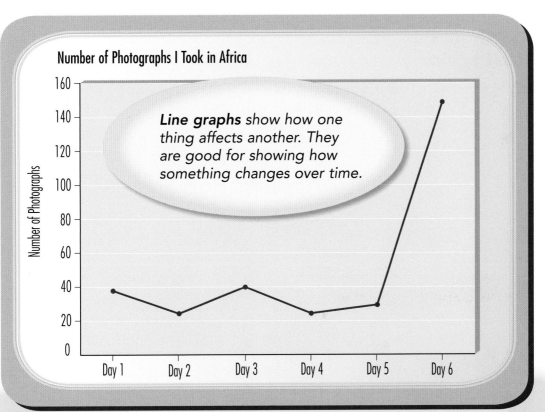

Number of Photographs I Took in Africa

Line graphs show how one thing affects another. They are good for showing how something changes over time.

Number of Photographs

Day 1, Day 2, Day 3, Day 4, Day 5, Day 6

Glossary

bar graph graph that uses rectangle-shaped bars to compare data. A bar graph helps you see which amount is largest or smallest.

data pieces of information. People who study animals collect data.

double bar graph graph that uses two bars to compare two kinds of data. Your double bar graph compared this year's cat count to last year's.

double line graph line graph that compares two sets of data. A double line graph shows two sets of data in one place.

graph picture that shows data. You turned your data into graphs.

horizontal flat. The surface of a table is horizontal.

label words that tell what part of a graph means. Without labels, graphs make no sense.

line graph graph that uses a line to show how one thing affects another. Line graphs often show how something changes over time.

pie chart graph showing what parts make up a whole. Each slice of a pie chart shows a different thing.

record write down. You watched the animals and recorded what you saw.

table chart that organizes data. You wrote your data down in tables.

tally mark line that stands for something you are counting. Tally marks are often written in groups of five.

vertical upright. A tree grows vertically.

Want to Know More?

Books to read

- Bader, Bonnie. *Graphs.* New York: Grosset & Dunlap, 2003.

- Long, Lynette. *Great Graphs and Sensational Statistics.* Hoboken, NJ: John Wiley & Sons, Inc., 2004.

- Underwood, Deborah. *Exploring Continents: Africa.* Chicago: Heinemann Library, 2007.

Websites

- http://nces.ed.gov/nceskids/createagraph/
  You can make your own graphs on this website.

- http://www.serengeti.org/
  Visit this website to learn more about the animals in this book.

Find out more about how animals live together in ***The War in Your Backyard***.

Read more about amazing animals in ***Animal Secrets***.

Index